with best.

for

Xmas and the

Coming Year

from

Mary & Holman

_____

Xmas 1952.

LINLITHGOW
IN PICTURES

ARMS ON THE WAIST OF "MEG DUNCAN,"
ONE OF THE BELLS IN ST. MICHAEL'S CHURCH

SEAL OF THE BURGH OF LINLITHGOW
(Obverse and Reverse)

MARY QUEEN OF SCOTS

Frontispiece   *Photo by Annan*

From the painting in the Kelvingrove Art Galleries,
Glasgow, and formerly in the Collection of the Earl of
Morton at Dalmahoy.

This portrait is said by the late Sir Lionel Cust to
be " the most pleasing presentation of Mary Stuart
extant."

LINLITHGOW
IN PICTURES

CONTAINING

TWENTY-FIVE FULL-PAGE AND THREE DOUBLE-
PAGE ILLUSTRATIONS, ALSO A PLAN, AS WELL
AS FIVE SMALLER ILLUSTRATIONS IN THE
PRELIMINARY PAGES

WITH AN INTRODUCTION BY
ANGUS MACDONALD, M.A.

A. & C. BLACK LTD.
4, 5 & 6 SOHO SQUARE, LONDON, W. 1

THE GATEWAY TO THE PALACE

PRINTED IN GREAT BRITAIN
AND PUBLISHED MAY 1932

PREFACE

ALL readers of books are aware how they can be carried away by their reading. It may interest those to know that the making of a book is no less fascinating. We who, in the wish to do something to help our native town, have nursed this book from its humble beginnings to its present state of completion, have become more and more interested in our labour of love, and it is almost with a feeling of regret that we come to the end of our self-appointed task. We have throughout been gratified with the cordiality with which dwellers in Linlithgow and others interested have volunteered their aid, and we take this opportunity of thanking them all, especially the following :—

EDINBURGH UNIVERSITY LIBRARY, for permission to reproduce prints from Slezer's *Theatrum Scotiae* and Wood's *Symbolae Scoticae.*

Mr. JAMES RUSSELL, Town Clerk of Linlithgow, for the plate of the Charter of 1389, and the photograph of Greenyards.

Mr. W. W. SPENCE, Linlithgow, for the Regent Moray print, Dick's *Monthly Advertiser,* the Burgh Seal, photographs of the David Waldie plaque, the Marches Day, and Alexander of Bonhard.

Mrs. JAMES DYMOCK, Royal Terrace, for a water-colour of Brockley's Land.

Mr. J. G. B. HENDERSON, Linlithgow, for a water-colour of Cornwall of Bonhard's House, and for a photograph of the Beinn-Castle Brae Houses.

Mr. T. S. VEITCH, Linlithgow, for Collie's " Linlithgow Palace " and Wood's plan.

Provost DOUGAL, Linlithgow, for Clark's view of the town.

Councillor JAMES BEVERIDGE, Linlithgow, for reading over the draft of the Introduction.

CONTENTS

CROWN ON TOWER OF ST. MICHAEL'S
CHURCH
(Removed 1821)

LIST OF ILLUSTRATIONS

9

SMALLER ILLUSTRATIONS

ST. MICHAEL'S WELL

NOTES ON THE SMALLER ILLUSTRATIONS
IN THE PRELIMINARY PAGES

Page 1. THE BURGH ARMS ON THE WAIST OF " MEG DUNCAN," THE
FIRST BELL IN ST. MICHAEL'S CHURCH (*from a rubbing*)

This is a Dutch bell, and probably cast at Amsterdam. On it is the
date 1718. It is interesting to note that the oldest bell in the church,
the " Alma Maria "—one of the largest mediæval bells in Scotland—
dates from 1490.

Page 2. THE BURGH SEAL (*obverse and reverse*).

The obverse is thus described in a record in the Lyon Office, dating
from *c.* 1673 : " The figur of the Arch-Angell Michaell, with
winges expanded tredding on ye bellie of a serpent . . . the head
of which he is pearceing through with a Spear in his dexter hand,
and grasping with his sinister ane Inescutcheon charged with the
Royall Armes of Scotland." Of the reverse we may remark that it
seems to be the older of the two, though it has been considerably
changed in form. One example of the seal, of 1357, shows the dog
chained to a ring on a pole. It is conjectured that the oak-tree
(*not* willow) was added at the Restoration, to commemorate the
escape of Charles II. from his enemies by hiding in an oak, and that
the motto, " My fruit is fidelity to God and the King," belongs
to the same period. Probably the black bitch is nothing more than
a symbol for the Royal hunts around Linlithgow, while the obverse
is probably due to the fact that the dedication of the Parish Church
is to St. Michael. The Royal Arms held by the Archangel signify
the Kings' residence in the Palace.

Page 6. THE GATEWAY TO THE PALACE.

Th's gateway bears the insignia of the four orders of knighthood
borne by James V.—The Golden Fleece, St. Michael, The Garter,
St. Andrew or The Thistle.
It was built before 1535, and the Order of the Thistle was instituted
in 1540, so that the original panels must have been inserted into an
existing structure. The panels have been frequently repaired, on
the last occasion at the beginning of the present century.

Page 8. CROWN OF THE TOWER OF ST. MICHAEL'S CHURCH.

> Five churches only in Scotland had a crown on top of the tower—
> St. Giles', Edinburgh; King's College, Aberdeen; the Old Tron
> Church, Glasgow; Haddington and Linlithgow. Of these, the first
> three may still be seen.

Page 10. ST. MICHAEL'S WELL.

> This well bears the date 1720, and the quaint inscription,
> "Saint Michael is kinde to Straingers."

LINLITHGOW IN PICTURES

FROM its geographical position alone, Linlithgow in the olden days was bound to be of almost vital importance. Situated as it is in the very centre of the plain which stretches through the middle of Scotland, it held the passage from the East to the West, just as Stirling held that to the Highlands. We cannot wonder, then, that the " Royal and Ancient Burgh " should have been the scene of many stirring contests for power in Scotland, when the kings had to rule by the strong arm, and had frequently to consolidate their power at the expense of a band of turbulent and unscrupulous nobles.

Whether it be the case or not that Linlithgow is the site of a Roman encampment—a theory which is quite feasible, if one considers its place on the map—it is at any rate fairly certain that it became a position of importance early in the traceable history of Scotland. We have evidence that David I. had a manor-house practically on the site of the present Palace, and though Linlithgow does not figure as a Royal Burgh in written documents till considerably later than this period, the fact that it, with Lanark, took the places of Roxburgh and Berwick, then in the hands of the English, in the Convention of the Four Burghs, in 1368, goes to prove that it had previously attained this dignity.

Before this time, even, it was the abode of the invading English under Edward I., who stayed here in 1301, and is wrongly supposed to be responsible for the small towers, if they can so be called, which may still be seen to the east of the majestic ruins of the Palace.   Edward I.'s castle, which was no doubt made of wood, with one part only of stone, was nevertheless considered of sufficient importance to merit a gallant and successful attempt to capture it for Bruce by one Binnock or Binning, about the year 1313.   Presumably it was levelled to the ground by Bruce, in accordance with his usual custom.   But it must have been soon rebuilt, as it figured in the fire of 1424, when the town, Palace, and Church were all burned down.   After this date, the Palace figures, not as a place of defence, but as the jointure house of the Queens of Scotland.

I do not purpose giving a detailed history of the Palace.   Suffice it to say that it was greatly altered during the reigns of James IV. and his son, James V., the latter of whom was born there, on 10th April 1512, and, later, by James VI., who rebuilt the north wing during the years 1617–1620, as the dates on that part of the Palace show. Probably the best-known fact about the Palace, however, is that the ill-fated Mary Queen of Scots was born in one of the rooms in the west wing there, on 8th December 1542.

Again, though it is possible that the east part of St. Michael's Church is older than 1424, the greater part of that edifice belongs to the first half of the sixteenth century.

The nature of the land round about Linlithgow must always have had a great amount of influence on the shape and growth of the town. No doubt it has grown from a small cluster of houses round the path to the manor-house, to a straggling street, running roughly east and west, and therefore following the line of the Loch. In the centre and hub of the town were the Cross and market-place, where all the business was transacted. Then, looking down on the romantic mediæval town, with its crow-stepped gables turned towards the street, there were the Palace, at that time " a princely dwelling," and the Church, heavy with the scent of incense from its six-and-twenty altars, and glittering with costly gifts from pious citizens. Linlithgow street in those days was even narrower, owing to the custom which existed of building outwards in wood, thus forming galleries and arcades in front. It is interesting to note that some of these galleries were still in existence at the beginning of the nineteenth century, as they are mentioned in the *Rambling Reminiscences* of Adam Dawson of Bonnytoun, a former Provost of the town.

The fifteenth and sixteenth centuries were the days of Linlithgow's greatness—when the old town had a thriving port of its own at Blackness, and the monopoly of trade between the rivers Avon and Almond. In 1596, during the reign of James VI., it was for some time the potential capital of Scotland ; while in 1646, owing to an outbreak of plague in Edinburgh, it was the seat of the Parliament and of Edinburgh University, the former being held in the Hall or Lyon Chamber of the Palace, and the latter in St. Michael's.

The sunshine that seemed during the seventeenth century to be gilding Linlithgow proved to be but a transitory gleam. With the rest of Scotland, its prosperity had been badly hurt by the removal of the Court to England. The most decisive blow, however, was dealt it by a neighbouring town—Bo'ness, which, by the influence of the

Duke of Hamilton, was erected into a Burgh of Regality in 1668, and thus was favoured by the Act of 1672, which allowed Burghs of Regality and Barony the liberty to export, import, and retail— an Act which deprived Linlithgow of her monopoly, and ruined Blackness. Writers of the eighteenth century who visited Blackness—for example, Bishop Pococke (1760) and Thomas Pennant (1772)—comment on the decay and lifelessness of the former flourishing port.

Bishop Pococke, an Englishman who became Bishop of Meath, twice toured Scotland, in 1747 and 1760. In the account of his second tour he gives what is really a tabloid history of the town, though we can hardly expect it to be accurate (I give the original spelling).

" We went on six miles [from Falkirk] to Linlithgow commonly called Lithgow, which consists of a street ; it may be three-quarters of a measured mile long : Here is the very handsome modern [sic] Gothic Church formerly belonging to the Palace which stands just before it ; it is hewn freestone inside and out, and remains much in the same way as it was fitted up at the Reformation, with the King's Semicircular Seat against a pillar opposite to the pulpit : There is a Chapel to the South, in which they say James 4th was attending

Vespers, and an old man came to him and desired him not to go to the battle against the English at Flodden Field, for that he would not return ; immediate search being made the old man could not be found, and 'tis supposed to have been a contrivance of the Queen's. I had no information of a Monastery founded for Carmelites in 1290 by the Citizens. The palace is built round a court, the south and west sides by James 5th, the north by James 6th. The parliament house is a fine room, the south end is all chimney, but divided into three below, by two pillars with Gothic Capitals adorned with foliage and above with two walls, at the north end is a musick gallery, & in the west side a gallery is practiced in the walls for the hearers, to the East are windows ; on the west side Mary Queen of Scots was born : In the middle was a fine fountain adorned with Statuary and Sculpture, but they say our Soldiers after the battle of Culloden destroyed it to get the lead ; and when they left it, burnt the palace as by accident ; it is situated in an Island on a Lough, a mile long, and a quarter of a mile broad."

Commenting on Pococke's account, we may note that the story about James IV. is to be found in Lindsay of Pitscottie's *Chronicles of Scotland*. Although the Bishop had no information of the

Carmelite Monastery, the ruins of this are in the grounds of Nether Parkley ; hence the modern names of Friars' Brae, Friars' Well. Pococke is suspicious, too, of the " accident " theory as to the burning of the Palace ; but such was the contemporary account, from the *Scots Magazine* for 1746 : " The ancient palace of Linlithgow was accidentally burned to the ground on the 1st of February. Soldiers were quartered in it the night before ; and it was feared they had not been careful enough of their fires." This laconic notice is the obituary of the birthplace of two Scottish monarchs and the residence of all of them from the time of Robert II. to James VI.

From the end of the fifteenth century till the Union of the Crowns in 1603, the history of Linlithgow is almost equivalent to a short history of Scotland. After that the burgh appears, unfortunately for it, only in connection with the wilder and more destructive aspects of history. Cromwell visited the town in 1651, and *his* accomplishments can be measured by the words of a charter of 1662, which granted the town the privilege of a three-days' fair free, " considering the great loss sustained by the burgh, and the destruction of all their public works by the attack of the usurper, viz., their church, hospital, school, market cross, tolbooth,

well, four mills and storehouses or granaries at
Blackness, so that they are laden with the burden for
restoring certain of said works and erecting afresh
the rest levelled with the ground." Likewise, the
visit of that romantic figure in Scottish history,
Prince Charles Edward, in 1746, probably caused
the destruction of the Palace. After the '45,
Linlithgow is glad to obtain a small degree of notice
through the reflected merit of Britain's great sons.
For example, Sir John Moore, the hero of the re-
treat to Corunna in 1809, was one M.P. for Linlithgow, when still plain Colonel John Moore.
This was in 1784, during which year he became a
Burgess of the Burgh—strange contrast with another
freeman and soldier, the Duke of Cumberland of
Culloden fame !

It is interesting to compare the description given
by the English clergyman with that of the Scottish
poet Robert Burns (a freeman of the town, 16th
November 1787), who visited Linlithgow in his
Highland tour of August 1787, and writes in his
Diary on the 25th of that month :

" Linlithgow, the appearance of rude, decayed,
idle grandeur, charmingly rural, retired situation.
The old rough palace a tolerably fine but melancholy
ruin—sweetly situated on a small elevation on the
brink of a loch. Shown the room where the

beautiful, injured Mary Queen of Scots was born—
A pretty good old Gothic church—the infamous stool
of repentance standing, in the old Romish way,
in a lofty situation.   What a poor, pimping business is a Presbyterian place of worship ! dirty,
narrow, squalid ; stuck in a corner of old popish
grandeur such as Linlithgow ! "

Notice the difference in the attitudes of
the two men—the antiquary and the poet—keen
observers both, but Burns with a warmer heart,
who, though somewhat annoyed at the " infamous
stool of repentance," thought of Mary Queen
of Scots, not as a moral lesson or a subject of
historical study, but as an injured and beautiful
woman.

Linlithgow during the ages had been mentioned in literature from the time of Wyntoun to
that of Scott ; the latter's *Marmion*, where he describes first of all the beautiful surroundings, then
the scene in St. Catherine's Aisle, is so familiar to
every one that I shall not venture to quote it.   But
for a prose description which would do full justice
to the peace and romance of the countryside it had
to wait for the *Dreamthorp* of a Kilmarnock lace-
pattern maker, Alexander Smith.

*Dreamthorp : A Book of Essays written in the
Country*, first appeared in 1863.   In the title essay

Smith describes, in the guise of an old schoolmaster, the town as he viewed it first, " with its westward-looking windows painted by sunset, its children playing in the single straggling street, the mothers knitting at the open doors, the fathers standing about in long white blouses, chatting or smoking ; the great tower of the ruined castle rising high into the rosy air, with a whole troop of swallows—by distance made as small as gnats—skimming about its rents and fissures."

And again : " Dreamthorp can boast of a respect-able antiquity, and in it the trade of the builder is unknown. Ever since I remember, not a single stone has been laid on the top of another. The castle, inhabited now by jackdaws and starlings, is old ; the chapel which adjoins it is older still ; and the lake behind both, and in which their shadows sleep, is, I suppose, as old as Adam. A fountain in the market-place, all mouths and faces and curious arabesques—as dry, however, as the castle moat—has a tradition connected with it ; and a great noble riding through the street one day several hundred years ago, was shot from a window by a man whom he had injured. The death of this noble is the chief link which connects the place with authentic history. The houses are old, and remote dates may yet be deciphered on the stones

above the doors ; the apple-trees are mossed and
ancient ;   countless generations of sparrows have
bred in the thatched roofs, and thereon have chirped
out their lives.   In every corner of the place men
have been born, men have died.   On Dreamthorp
centuries have fallen, and have left no more trace
than have last winter's snowflakes.''

The tradition in connection with the fountain to
which Smith refers may possibly be the fact that,
at least during the visit of the Young Pretender,
it ran wine.

The great noble he mentions was the Regent
Moray, who was shot, as he was riding through the
street of Linlithgow on 23rd January 1569–70,
by James Hamilton of Bothwellhaugh.   It was long
supposed that the motive for the crime was revenge,
since Hamilton's wife was believed to have died of
exposure after having been evicted from her home
at the instigation of the Regent.   Recent research,
however, has proved this story to be as unreliable
as that of King Alfred and the cakes.

To-day we live in an age of machinery and of
bustle, which have penetrated into and greatly
changed even Smith's Dreamthorp.   Yet although
the old crow-stepped gables have mostly disappeared,
to be replaced by modern if much uglier edifices,
it is still possible to discover traces of the long-past

days of Linlithgow's greatness, and to see in un-expected nooks and crannies hidden beauties of adornment, which we wish both the inhabitants of the town and those who are but strangers within our gates to share with us.

ALEXANDER OF BONHARD (see page 32)

No. 2. CHARTER BY ROBERT II. IN FAVOUR OF THE BURGH

From a photograph in the Old Town Hall, Linlithgow, presented by the late John Ferguson, Town Clerk

THE CHARTER, WHICH IS DATED 23RD OCTOBER 1389, HAS BEEN TRANSLATED AS FOLLOWS :—

" Robert, by the grace of God, King of Scots, to all worthy men of his whole land, clerics and laymen, wisheth health ; Know ye that we have granted and at ferme dimitted to our lovite and faithful burgesses and community of our Burgh of Lynlithcu, our Burgh aforesaid, together with the haven of Blaknes, the fermes of the Burgh, and petty customs and toll dues, with courts, and the issues of courts, and other just pertinents whatsoever : To be holden and had to our said burgesses and community aforesaid, and their successors, for ever, with all their pertinents above mentioned, in fee and heritage, as is above expressed : Paying therefor to us and our heirs, the said burgesses and community and their successors, into our royal exchequer, five pounds of sterlings every year, and at the usual terms.

" In Witness of which thing, to this our present Charter we have commanded our Seal to be set : Witnesses, the venerable fathers in Christ : Walter, Bishop of Saint Andrews, and John, Bishop of Dunkeld our Chancellor ; John Earl of Carric, Steward of Scotland, our firstborn, Robert Earl of Fyfe and Menteith, our beloved son, George Earl of March, our kinsman ; Archibald of Douglas and Thomas of Erskyne our beloved kinsmen, Knights ; At Lithcu, the twenty third day of October, and of our reign the eighteenth year."

R R

Robtus dei gra Rex Scottorum Omnibus
concessimus et ad firma dimisimus burgensibz a
... bna ar portu de blaknes firma burgi et f
ptiue^ quibuscu^ tene^d esstend eisdm br
omnibus sine prive^ guidas in feodo a hredi
... cora siue a dues
consuetis ... sie ... in testiom psenti cart
Wato a iestmi ... ... standi a dunkeldon
de fifo a ad seneth filie ... dicto ... Georen
ma de eysstemo ... ... dicto ... anth
de lesmo :.

omnibz tenens ... libas potum gaue ...
qui ... de huikeich ditu ... fidelibz ... custum ... pot
stanub ac tolonens ... anno ... capioz ... a code mstibi
... et conuem phus ... corp cracessdub ...
... ... Soluendo undo nob ...
... ... tinxory annus ... ...
... ... sigilt Testibz bed. in ...
... epis ... pruoz ... ...
... constuig ... achebat de Jongebs ...
... biastmo ... dio dcotz Anno regni ...

No. 3.   THE DOVECOT

THIS is the only circular dovecot in West Lothian, and dates back probably to the sixteenth century. It belonged to the noble family of Ross of Halkhead. There may still be seen in it the ledges on which the pigeons nested. The richer families in Scotland during the Middle Ages found pigeons a welcome variation from salted meat, the usual winter fare in those days.

No. 4. THE HOUSE FROM WHICH THE REGENT MORAY WAS SHOT

From an engraving by Ph. de la Motte

THIS house occupied part of the site where the Sheriff Court House now stands. The engraving may only represent the rebuilt or restored house, as the tradition is, that the original "incontinent thairefter wes all utterlie burnt with fyre." Even since de la Motte made the engraving, the house must have been considerably altered. A prominent Linlithgow townsman, lecturing in 1897, stated that when it was taken down it was discovered that a wall had been built 10 feet forward to the line of the street, and the intervening space filled up with rooms. Some of the stumps of the beams of the old balcony, presumably that from which the Regent was shot, had evidently escaped the fire, and still remained in the wall; this gentleman had them extracted, and sent one to Mr. Glencairn Hamilton of Dalziel, the representative of Hamilton of Bothwellhaugh.

No. 5. THE TOWN HOUSE OF CORNWALL
OF BONHARD

From a water-colour by J. Etherington Cook·,
1863

THE site of this house was almost thirty yards to the
west of the present office of the Commercial Bank.
The ceilings of the building were elaborately decorated
with stucco work, and the centre ornament of one of
the rooms was the head of Alexander, the hero of the
family, who fell at Flodden. It is said that, at the
battle, he was one of the six knights dressed in the same
style as the King, whom he much resembled.

The centre ornament referred to is now in the
possession of a well-known Linlithgow family.

A stone bearing the Cornwall arms, with the inscription, " VE BIG YE SE VARLY, 1527," may still be
seen built into the back of the house, No. 59 High
Street.

No. 6. BROCKLEY'S LAND

From a water-colour by A. S. Boyd, 1885

THE Victoria (Jubilee) Hall now stands here, and a tablet in the entrance informs us that the site was presented by Miss Jessie D. Baird to commemorate her brother, Dr. George Dallas Baird, who practised for about fifty years in the town and neighbourhood.

No. 7. OLD HOUSES—40-48 HIGH STREET

THESE date from the late sixteenth or the seventeenth century. Notice the crow-stepped gables still in good preservation. They were built by the Hamiltons of Pardovan and Humbie.

No. 8. OLD HOUSES ON BEINN-CASTLE BRAE

THE house with the outside stair and the two to the left of it were demolished by the Town Council in 1930–1931. They were built about the middle of the seventeenth century. The high house on the extreme right, West Port House, has belonged to a cadet of the Hamiltons of Silvertonhill, in Lanarkshire, since the seventeenth century at least—the house being completed in 1600, when James Hamilton of West Port was the owner. It shows traces of later alterations.

No. 9. THE GOLDEN CROSS TAVERN

THE attic of this house is believed to be the room in which Robert Burns became a member of the local Masonic Lodge, in 1787, when on a visit to his friend, James Smith, then working the Avon Print Mill at Linlithgow Bridge.

The arms on the front of the house are probably those of one James Craufurd, with the date 1675.

No. 10. GREENYARDS

A SEVENTEENTH-CENTURY building which stood on the site of the present Post Office.

Nos. 11 AND 12. SLEZER'S VIEWS OF TOWN AND PALACE

THESE are from a collection of prints called " *Theatrum Scotiae*, containing the Prospects of Their Majesties Castles and Palaces, etc., by John Slezer, Captain of the Artillery Company, and Surveyor of Their Majesties' Stores and Magazines in the Kingdom of Scotland. Printed in London, 1693."

Slezer was a Dutchman, who settled in Scotland in 1669. Through his proficiency as a draughtsman, he became acquainted with several of the nobility, and through their influence was appointed a lieutenant of artillery, with the practical superintendence of the ordnance. About 1678 he began his series of etchings of the King's " Castles, Pallaces, towns, and other notable places in the kingdom belonging to private subjects," for that purpose travelling widely through Scotland. He died in 1714.

Prominent in both of the prints is the Town Hall, which was built in 1668–1670, during the provostship of Sir Robert Miles of Barnton, and burned down in 1847, the present Old Town Hall being completed the following year, when Adam Dawson of Bonnytoun was Provost. Two relics of the Hall will be found in the Burgh Museum—the weathercock from the steeple, and a hand of the clock. It will be noticed also that St. Michael's Church has a crown on its tower, like St. Giles in Edinburgh at the present day. This crown was removed from the tower of the Parish Church of Linlithgow about 1821, since it was feared that the tower could not support its weight—a quite unnecessary precaution.

Prospectus Civitatis LIMNUCHI .

Prospect of the Town of LINLITHGOW.

Prospectus Regis Palatis LIMNUCHENSIS.

Prospect of Their Maj.^ties Palace of LINLITHGOW.

No. 13. THE PALACE AND TOWN FROM SOUTH-EAST

From an engraving by W. R. Smith of the picture by A. W. Calcott, R.A.

THIS view seems to have been taken from a little to the east of the present St. Magdalene's Distillery, and, as the crown is still shown on the church spire, the date must be prior to 1821. The canal, apparently complete on the left, was not open to traffic till 1822. A number of men appear to be at work on the bank.

No. 14. "THE TOWN OF LINLITHGOW, DRAWN ON THE SPOT BY J. CLARK"

From an engraving published by Smith & Elder, London, in 1824

THE view is taken from the north-west of the town. One of the figures in the foreground is believed to be a local personage called Gibbeson, the other the farmer on whose land they were.

No. 15.   LINLITHGOW PALACE FROM SOUTH-WEST

From the illustration in " The Royal Palace of Linlithgow," by J. Collie, published by Adam & Charles Black, circa 1840

THIS shows the south gate built by James V., also the wall extending from the west wing of the Palace southward, which was taken down when the present keeper's house was built.

To the extreme east of the south wing of the Palace is the Chapel, with the mitre carved above the door, its choir gallery, and niches for saints. This is mentioned in records frequently about the end of the fifteenth century, when it seems to have been in course of construction.

DICK'S
MONTHLY ADVERTISER

For LINLITHGOWSHIRE, and the   Eastern District of STIRLINGSHIRE.

No. 16. REDUCED FACSIMILE OF A PAGE OF
DICK'S MONTHLY ADVERTISER

This was a newspaper published at the price of one
penny by George Hay Dick, Printer, Bookseller, and
Stationer, 293 High Street, Linlithgow. Its last
number, No. 87, appeared on 7th December 1847—
the reasons for its failure being the rise of the *Falkirk
Herald*, which took away the Stirlingshire trade, and
the then overwhelming tax on newspapers. At its
height of publication it had a circulation of not less
than 800, and rising to 1200 a month. Copies we
have seen of the paper are made up thus : Front page,
advertisements, and perhaps a special article, as that
on the journey of Queen Victoria and Prince Albert
into Scotland ; second page, local news, such as the
progress of the (then) new Town Hall, local concerts,
or accounts of the proceedings of the Sheriff Court.
The rest of the paper is taken up with moral tales or
what the age considered to be interesting facts, and
the last page, again advertisements—of replenishing
sales, farms to let, and so on.

Mr. Dick emigrated to Australia in 1851. He
returned to Scotland in 1857 and resided in Bathgate.

HERITABLE SUBJECTS IN LINLITHGOW FOR SALE.

To be Sold by Public Roup, within the House of JOHN ADAMS, Innkeeper at Cross of Linlithgow, on THURSDAY, 23d December current, at Two o'clock afternoon, in virtue of the powers of Sale contained in an Heritable Bond,

ALL and WHOLE the HERITABLE SUBJECTS situated at WEST PORT of the Burgh of LINLITHGOW, which are described in the Title-Deeds thereof as follows, viz.:—All and Whole that Tenement of Land, high and laigh, back and fore, with the Yard and Pertinents thereto belonging, lving within the Burgh of Linlithgow, at the West Port thereof, upon the South side of the High Street, bounded by the Tenement sometime of Margaret Nicol, thereafter of Thomas White, and now of his Heirs, on the East ; the Tenement sometime of the Heirs of William Spence, now of Thomas Brown, on the West ; the Lands sometime of the Heirs of James Couper, now of William Hamilton, Esq of West Port, on the South ; and the King's High Street on the North parts, all as said Subjects were sometime possessed by the deceased Duncan M'Farlane, vintner in Linlithgow, afterwards by the also deceased Mrs Mary Baird or M'Farlane, his Widow, and now by their Heirs.

The Subjects are capable of affording a vote in the Burgh of Linlithgow.

The Title-Deeds and Articles of Roup are with Mr JOHN HARDY, writer, Linlithgow.

Linlithgow, 7th December 1847.

COALS.

WILLIAM & JOHN WILSON,
STANDRIG COLLIERY,

BEG to inform the Inhabitants of LINLITHGOW and the surrounding country, that they have opened a COAL-YARD at the Town of LINLITHGOW, where the Public can now be supplied with very Superior SPLINT COAL, at the rate of 8s. 9d. per Ton, and Rich SOFT COAL, at the rate of 9s. 3d. per Ton.

The excellent quality of these Coals have been long known to the Public, and W. & J. W consider it unnecessary here to give them any farther recommendation.

The place of Sale being now so convenient to Linlithgow, as well as to Farmers and others in the neighbourhood, they rely with confidence on having an extensive share of business.

The Coal-yard is near the Teind Barn, between the Railway and Canal.

Orders carefully attended to.

Tickets are always given when required.

Standrig Colliery, 1st December 1847.

LOCAL NEWS.

THE TOWN-HOUSE.

Since our last publication, the Town Council and the county gentlemen have come to terms as to the sums they are respectively to bear in repairing the Town-house, and the accommodation which the county courts are to have therein. This is all as it ought to be ; and we would, therefore, hope and expect, from the good taste of the committees of both bodies, aided by the architect they have agreed on—Mr Thomas Brown—that we shall have a more commodious interior than ever.

LINLITHGOW PAROCHIAL BOARD—YEAR ENDING SEPTEMBER 1847.

Abstracts of the accounts of the Inspector and Collector have been lately printed, and circulated among the members; as also, a list of the persons who have received aid from the funds during the bypast year. From these documents the following facts are made known :—

That the Parish was assessed in the sum of £885, 9s 3d, and that a benevolent gentleman sent £10 in aid of the funds—that £661, 10s 11d was paid to paupers on the permanent roll—that £136, 10s 3½d was paid as temporary relief—£40 for coals to the poor—£11, 1s for coffins and funeral expenses for do.—£8, 1s 6d for clothing for do.—£17, 14s 5d for education for do.—£16, 5s 8d for medicine, cordials, and nutritious diet for do.—£117, 3s 4d for salaries—and £15, 5s 7d for miscellaneous charges, embracing printing, stationery, postages, and a great variety of other

items. These sums amount to more than £1000; so that the assessment is noways able to meet the expenditure. This we know is gone about in as frugal a manner as possible. During the last year no less than 211 persons were on the permanent roll of paupers, 21 of whom died. There were 4 lunatics kept in asylums, at a charge of from £18 to £23 each per annum, one of whom died. A sprinkling of illegitimate children are on the funds too. The latter cost the Board a good deal of annoyance, chiefly arising from the difficulties of compelling the male parents to pay the mother—denial of paternity, &c. &c. These are evils in this wicked world of ours, which, as they cannot be cured, must just be endured.

SHERIFF COURT TRIALS.

Yesterday, four criminal cases came before Mr Sheriff CAY ; the first, a case of simple theft—the second, theft and previous conviction—the third, theft, by housebreaking, and previous conviction—and the last, assault, with intent to ravish.

1. John Tullis, a young boy of about 12 years of age, pled guilty to a charge of stealing a silver watch, a gold seal, a watch key and ribbon, the property of Alexander Gray, weaver, Broxburn. The juvenile delinquent, after a proper admonition from the Sheriff, was sentenced to 4 months' imprisonment.

2. Robert Forrester or Forster, a man of about 35 years of age, and an old offender, pled guilty to a charge of stealing a pair of spectacles and a case from Mrs Fraser, wife of Mr William Fraser, innkeeper, Broxburn. Three previous convictions were libelled on, and admitted. The Sheriff sentenced Forrester to 3 months' imprisonment.

3. Hugh M'Coll, aged about 25, was charged with breaking into Binns Easter Lodge, and stealing therefrom a great quantity of men's wearing apparel, the property of George Neuton, railway-surfaceman, aggravated by his having been previously convicted of theft. M'Coll pled not guilty. A jury having been sworn and empanelled, and proof led, which clearly established the offence charged against him, he was found guilty as libelled by an unanimous verdict, and received sentence of 12 months' imprisonment in Perth Penitentiary.

4. The last case was tried with closed doors. Owen Mullane, a railway labourer, was charged with assaulting a widow woman, aged 60, of the name of Margaret M'Intosh or Manly, within her own dwelling-house at Kirkliston, on the night of 22d October last, and with intent to ravish her. Mullane pled not guilty. The old woman herself, a number of her neighbours, and a medical gentleman (Dr Braid) proved the case. Mr Hardy made an able defence for the pannel. After a lengthened summing up by the learned Sheriff, the jury, on a short consultation, unanimously found Mullane guilty, whereupon the Sheriff sentenced him, also, to 12 months in Perth Penitentiary. The Sheriff characterised this as a very atrocious case—and with great justice.

Mr Watson, the procurator-fiscal, conducted all the prosecutions in his usual correct manner. The court did not break up till half-past eight o'clock at night.

MR TEMPLETON.

This distinguished vocalist favoured the good folks of Linlithgow and vicinity with one of his entertainments on the evening of Friday, the 19th ult., in the County Hall. He was accompanied by the venerable Blewitt, who presided at the pianoforte. The programme or bill of fare comprehended four Scotch songs, viz., ' O, let me in this ae nicht,' ' Lass, gin ye lo'e me, tell me now,' ' The lea rig,' and ' The brisk young lad —three English, viz., ' The lads of the village,' ' Sally in our alley,' and Incledon's favourite sea song, ' The heaving of the lead'—two he picked up in America, ' Sally St Clair' and ' On de brown shores of Arkansas'—and two of Tom Moore's, ' The meeting of the waters' and ' They may rail at this life.' To say that the whole were sung in an unequalled style would be fulsome praise ; but it must be conceded by all who heard him that the singing and acting of his Scotch pieces—for example, ' The brisk young lad'—kept pace with his former most successful efforts. The Hall was well filled, and Blewitt finished with ' The merry little fat grey man,' amidst roars of laughter. Mr Templeton was evidently at the beginning not in good voice—a kind of huskiness. As he got on it cleared up, and he finished in grand style. The County Hall was handsomely granted for the occasion by Mr Stewart of Binny, convener, and other authorities—to whom many thanks are due for this and similar instances of accommodation for public assemblies.

No. 17. LINLITHGOW FROM THE SOUTH-EAST

Photo by Valentin

THIS illustration shows on the left the black tower-like building popularly known as " The Mint " (taken down 1885), which was really a residence of the Knights of St. John of Jerusalem, whose headquarters were at Torphichen. There will also be seen, to the right of St. Michael's Church, the Burgh School, which was burned down in February 1902. This school replaced an older building, a large one-roomed building to the east of the present County Hall, and this in turn replaced an older two-roomed building. In Adam Dawson of Bonnytoun's interesting book, *Rambling Recollections of Past Times* (1868), he describes this school, and how, till 1802, every year on " Fastern's E'en " there was held in the Grammar School a grand cock-fight.

The pupils at this or some previous school on the site included Patrick Hamilton, who was burned at the stake at St. Andrews in 1528, and Henry Forrest, who was also burned there about five years later. Their names are to be found on the Martyrs' Monument in St. Andrews.

No. 18. CROSS WELL AND OLD TOWN HALL

Photo by Valentine

THIS view will be unknown to many of the present generation of inhabitants, for the " Piazza " which formed the front of the Town Hall disappeared about 1906, to be replaced by the present double staircase. A door to the left gave entrance to the prison, now part of the Fire Station. The fountain in its present state dates from 1807, being built by Robert Gray, a one-handed mason from Edinburgh. The original fountain on that site was built about 1540, and re-built about 1630 and in 1659, it having been damaged by Cromwell's soldiers. Cross House, on the left, possesses several finely carved ceilings.

No. 19. CENTENARY MEMORIAL TABLET TO DR. DAVID WALDIE

THIS was erected on the house in Linlithgow (No. 67 High Street) where he resided and had his laboratory. The inscription on it reads thus :—

DAVID WALDIE

SURGEON L.R.C.S.E. AND CHEMIST
MEMBER OF ASIATIC SOC. BENGAL
B. LINLITHGOW 1818 D. CALCUTTA 1889
A PIONEER IN ANÆSTHETIC RESEARCH
TO HIM BELONGS THE DISTINCTION
OF HAVING BEEN THE FIRST TO
RECOMMEND AND MAKE PRACTICABLE
THE USE OF CHLOROFORM IN THE
ALLEVIATION OF HUMAN SUFFERING

DAVID WALDIE
SURGEON L·R·C·S·E· AND CHEMIST
MEMBER OF ASIATIC SOC· BENGAL
B· LINLITHGOW 1813 D· CALCUTTA 1889·
A PIONEER IN ANÆSTHETIC RESEARCH
TO HIM BELONGS THE DISTINCTION
OF HAVING BEEN THE FIRST TO
RECOMMEND AND MAKE PRACTICABLE
THE USE OF CHLOROFORM IN THE
ALLEVIATION OF HUMAN SUFFERING

No. 20. THE MARCHES DAY

VIEW of the procession on the annual excursion of riding the Marches or boundaries of the town—a celebration which takes place on " the first Tuesday after the second Thursday " of June. The burgesses, craftsmen, and other inhabitants are duly warned of this peregrination on the previous Friday, by tuck of drum and the proclamation by the town's crier, the penalty for absence being one hundred pounds Scots. After the " fencing of the marches " is over, the Magistrates and Town Council, attended by the various Crafts, each headed by its Deacon, and with the Society of Dyers (the oldest in Scotland) bringing up the rear, move towards Linlithgow Bridge, the western boundary of the town's power. On their return, they go to Blackness, where they hold a Barony Court, and elect a Bailie for their Barony of Blackness—now a purely honorary and not at all arduous post ! With the return to Linlithgow and the passage of the procession round the Cross Well, the great day ends.

The statue which appears in the illustration is that erected to John Adrian Louis Hope (1860–1908), seventh Earl of Hopetoun and First Marquis of Linlithgow, also First Governor - General of the Australian Commonwealth.

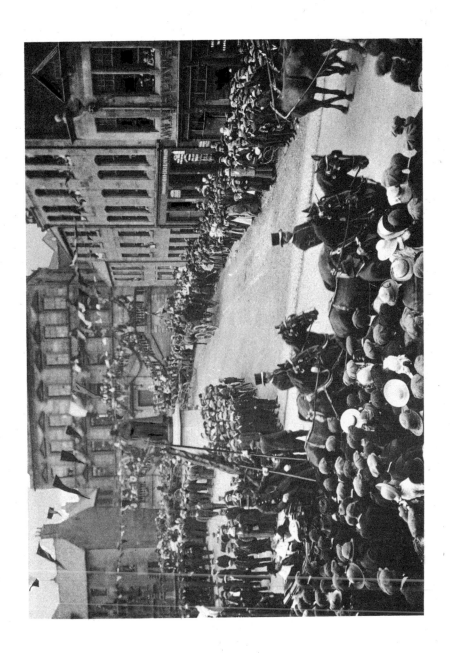

No. 21. AERIAL VIEW OF LINLITHGOW

Photo by Valentine

TAKEN from the south-west. About two-thirds of the town can be seen, as well as the Union Canal and the Edinburgh Road, while the promontory on which stand the Palace and Church is conspicuous.

No. 22.   THE PALACE FROM THE EAST

Photo by Valentine

HERE can be seen the gateway which was used previous to the building of the South Gateway by James V. Above the East Gateway are the Royal Arms, while at closer range there may be seen the holes for the chains of the drawbridge, and, inside, the opening for the portcullis. The circular towers in front date from the sixteenth century. The main feature of the East Wing is the Parliament Hall or Lyon Chamber, with its huge southern fireplace, formerly painted in oils the colours of which were still visible as late as 1860.

No. 23. QUADRANGLE OF PALACE FROM
NORTH-WEST

Photo by Valentine

THIS shows both the East and South entrances to the
Palace. Above the South Gateway there is to be
seen the remains of a group of statuary representing
the Salutation of the Virgin : the angel figure has
disappeared, but the effigy of the Virgin still stands
beside the pot of lilies. Above the East Gateway
was another group, representing the Nobility, Church,
and Commons. From the fountain in the centre of
the courtyard that at Holyrood was copied.

No. 24. QUADRANGLE OF PALACE FROM
SOUTH-EAST

Photo by Valentine

THE window in the middle of the West Wing, on the
left of the illustration, is probably that of the room in
which Mary Queen of Scots was born. The long
horizontal window to its right was made to let light
fall upon a beautifully painted ceiling. At the top of
the North-West tower is the room known as Queen
Margaret's Bower, where the wife of James IV. is
supposed to have watched for the return of her
husband after Flodden. The North Wing, to the
right, dates from the seventeenth century, and replaced an earlier wing which fell down in 1607. It
was in this part that the disastrous fire of 1746 first
began : consequently it is in a more ruinous condition
than the rest of the Palace. A feature of the wing is
the profusion of decoration above the windows.

No. 25. ST. MICHAEL'S CHURCH FROM SOUTH
Photo by Valentine

A GOTHIC, pre-Reformation structure, dating mostly from the latter part of the fifteenth century. It was "cleansed" by the Lords of the Congregation on 29 June 1559, and was distinguished by Cromwell by acting during his stay as stables. The statue of St. Michael, to whom the church was dedicated, is still in a niche on a buttress to the south-west of the church. Below the south window is the vault of the Livingstones, Earls of Linlithgow and Callendar, whose estates and titles were forfeited as a result of their participation on the Jacobite side in the Rebellion of 1715. Above the vault stands a mortsafe, which was removed from a grave at the recent restoration of the churchyard, and which serves as a gruesome relic of the days of Burke and Hare.

No. 26. INTERIOR OF ST. MICHAEL'S CHURCH FROM WEST

Photo by Valentine

ON the left may be seen the Royal Pew, and on the right, almost opposite, is St. Catherine's Aisle, where James IV., before Flodden, saw the vision, the story of which has been told so well by Sir Walter Scott in " David Lindsay's Tale " in *Marmion*. Beside the entrance to St. Catherine's Aisle is the tombstone of John Forrest of Magdelan, provost of Linlithgow (d. 159—), and his son-in-law, Robert Steuart (d. 1615)—remarkable in this, that it is one of some half-dozen in Scotland where the lettering runs round the stone. Other examples are in St. Andrews.

The church was restored during the years 1894–6, and reopened for worship in 1897. During these years a valiant attempt was made to repair as much as possible the damage which had been done in 1813, when the choir arch was removed, and a screen wall erected one bay to the east. The galleries which had disfigured the east end of the church—that which had been used—were taken down, and the choir arch restored. But it was impossible to replace the fine oak roof which had adorned the apse, and was removed, because of its decayed condition, in 1802.

76

No. 27. LINLITHGOW BRIDGE, WITH VIADUCT

Photo by Valentine

THE bridge in the foreground, crossing the River Avon and joining West Lothian and Stirlingshire, dates only from near the end of the nineteenth century, but it was preceded by a seventeenth-century structure built by the Earls of Linlithgow, who, to compensate them for the expenses incurred, were empowered to levy tolls at the bridge. This right was acquired about 1680 by the Town Council of the Burgh of Linlithgow, who exercised it for two hundred years, when in 1880, in consideration of the sum of £950 paid them by the two counties concerned, they resigned their interest in the bridge, which was then declared free.

While cutting was going on for the passage of the railway, the viaduct of which is seen in the background, evidence was found of the site of the battle of Linlithgow Bridge (1526), an attempt to get James V. out of the hands of the Douglases. The sword of the Earl of Lennox, who lost his life in this battle, can be seen in the Burgh Museum.

The viaduct is by the great engineer, Robert Telford.

No. 28.   BLACKNESS CASTLE AND VILLAGE

Photos by Valentine

BLACKNESS, at one time the port of Linlithgow, and
the seat of considerable trade, is now merely a quiet
little seaside village.

The oldest part of Blackness Castle dates from the
fifteenth century.   But with its acquisition by the
Crown in the sixteenth century, extensive alterations
were made, from which (roughly) has arisen the
present structure, shaped like a ship.   It has served
many uses—as castle, prison—it held many State
prisoners, including ministers imprisoned for their
religious beliefs during the seventeenth century—then
degraded to being used as a powder magazine.   It is
commonly believed that Blackness Castle is provided
for in the provisions of the Treaty of Union of 1707.
Actually, it is not mentioned at all !

No. 29. PLAN OF LINLITHGOW

BY JOHN WOOD, 1820

THIS is interesting in that it gives the names of the then owners of property in the town. A century has caused many changes, and it will be found that very few of the names are now represented locally.